Cape Fear
Ferry Tales

by Larry Modlin

To Andy
Hope to see you on the ferry.
Happy Father's Day

Best Wishes

Larry Modlin

SlapDash Publishing, LLC
Hampstead, North Carolina

Cape Fear Ferry Tales

by Larry Modlin

SlapDashPublishing.

625 Hickory Point Road, Hampstead, NC 28443
910.232.0604 • slapdashpub@me.com
www.carolinabeach.net

LIBRARY OF CONGRESS CONTROL NUMBER: **2018932037**
Larry Modlin
Cape Fear Ferry Tales
Hampstead, N.C., SlapDash Publishing, LLC.
100 pp.

International Standard Book Number: **978-0-9984115-2-1**
Copyright © 2018 Larry Modlin | First Printing: **March 2018** | Designed & Printed in the USA.
Photo credits: Larry Modlin, Daniel Ray Norris

NORTH CAROLINA SOUTHPORT-FORT FISHER FERRY ROUTE

NEW HANOVER COUNTY

CAROLINA BEACH

CAPE FEAR RIVER

FORT FISHER

BRUNSWICK COUNTY

SOUTHPORT

FERRY ROUTE

OAK ISLAND

Atlantic Ocean

BALD HEAD ISLAND

Cape Fear

N

Contents

About the Author

Larry Modlin

Larry Thomas Modlin spent his childhood in the small northeastern North Carolina town of Jamesville, in Martin County. He went to East Carolina University and began his adult life in the garment industry. He moved to Brunswick County to become a nuclear power plant operator, and then a public works director. During the late eighties, he even worked as a movie stunt man at De Laurentiis Entertainment Group studios with the International Stunt Association. As the years passed and the miles took their toll, Larry decided to share his recent experience with the NCDOT Ferry Division, in print. This little book is the result.

His family members are spread all along the eastern U.S. Atlantic coast. His favorite authors are Carl Hiaasen, Pat Conroy, John D. Mac-Donald, and Celia Rivenbark. Larry knows that life has given him many stories to tell. He hopes to continue his love of writing and storytelling.

My deepest gratitude goes out to Daniel Ray Norris and Mary Russ at SlapDash Publishing. Without their guidance and friendship, this project would not have come to be. If for no other reason, my attempt to bring you this book brought Daniel and Mary into my world. For that I will be eternally grateful.

Dedication

I WOULD LIKE TO DEDICATE THIS LITTLE STORYBOOK TO:

THE CREWS OF THE M/V *SOUTHPORT* AND THE M/V *FORT FISHER*, ALONG WITH THE SUPPORT STAFF AND MANAGE-MENT AT FORT FISHER LANDING AND THE SOUTHPORT LANDING TERMINAL.

I WOULD ALSO LIKE TO EXTEND A SINCERE THANK YOU TO EVERY MEMBER OF THE NORTH CAROLINA FERRY SYS-TEM THAT HAS SERVED, BOTH PAST AND PRESENT. YOU ARE PROVIDING A SERVICE AND AN EXPERIENCE, THAT THE STATE OF NORTH CAROLINA SHOULD BE PROUD OF.

Chapter 1

The Reason

At the age of 59 years, I found myself looking for a job. I was not the only one doing this at this time, due to our country's changing economic times. People my age, and younger, were being "let go" due to certain job skills no longer being needed. Robotics, foreign trade, economics, politics, and other factors, were all combining to make the older worker worth less than ever before in American history. But enough of the negative. It was not time to dwell on why. It was time to find employment that would fulfill my needs.

Now, I want to set the stage for this story by sharing how I got a job as a deckhand with the North Carolina Department of Transportation Ferry Division. Like many people, I needed health insurance until I reached Medicare age. I also desired to have a job that would provide some level of dignity while helping to improve the lives of others. I refused to play the retirement card, yet I was no longer the young guy that was able to physically push my limits on a daily basis. I was hopeful that I would find a job that paid above minimum wage. Thank the good Lord that I had not buried myself in debt. I had started financially planning my coast down to retirement, but that exit ramp would not be used just yet.

I live near the North Carolina Ferry System's route between Southport, NC and Fort Fisher, just south of Kure Beach, NC. It is a thirty minute crossing of the Cape Fear River. A friend of mine, Captain Harry Sell, had spent his entire career with the NC Ferry System. I had grown

up using many of the NC Ferry boats to travel between the islands and land masses of the Outer Banks of North Carolina. My thought was that this job with the NC Ferry Division would provide all of my needs for a new gig that would get me to my target age.

After spending roughly $350.00 to acquire the necessary credentials, I applied for a position as deckhand at the Southport terminal. I acquired the US Coast Guard Merchant Marine Credentials, the Transportation Workers Identification Card, and passed the required drug screening test. I felt as though I reached a new low by having to pay for my own drug test. Yet, everyone applying has to do this. If you get hired, they will give you all the drug tests you can stand, completely free. WOW! I say this as a joke. This job is definitely not the place to be chemically affected. Besides, I have been drug testing at every job since I began a nuclear career in 1982. Remember that Nancy Reagan told us all to just say NO!

I worked about nine months as a "Pool" employee, which is basically part-time, as needed, without benefits. During this period, you get to work on both ferries, and with all four crews. When the opportunity arose, I became a full time employee with benefits. Seven days on and seven days off, twelve and a half hours per day. This schedule is a little better suited to a 30 year old and not a 60 year old. But it was time to pull up the big boy pants and carry on. I was assigned to the M/V (motor vessel) *Southport* under the command of Captain Marybeth Ray. I had hoped to be assigned to this crew due to my previous work with them, and the reputation they have. I was lucky and I knew it. All of the daily commuter traffic that rode the ferry were extremely fond of this crew. I was going to try to do my best and not tarnish that reputation.

I have written this book to share interesting facts about the ferry and the people I have met. I have enjoyed the daily interaction with passengers and life on the water. This job provides a never ending study of sociology and human psyche. I am blessed by being able to talk to people from everywhere on the planet and from all walks of life.

The tales in this book are true. For the sake of dignity, and to avoid any embarrassment, names and dates will be avoided for the most part. If someone's name is used, it will be only to their honor. I will not use fake names without telling you, and only for the reasons I have mentioned. I will not be disparaging someone or adding to the story, just to create drama or comedy. I'll leave that to the politicians. I hope to make you laugh. It would make me feel good to know that I have taught the reader something about the NC Ferry System and our Cape Fear region. My greatest reward would be to think I have opened your eyes, minds, and hearts, to people and places that had not touched you before. Laugh loud, and love hard. Remember that I am just a human like the rest of you, riding this rock around the sun.

Chapter 2

The
Ferry Boats

There are two ferry boats currently assigned to the Cape Fear route. They are the M/V *Southport* and the M/V *Fort Fisher*. The NC Ferry System adorns all of its vessels with an affiliated university in North Carolina. I cannot explain how certain boats get certain university affiliations. Someone above my pay grade makes those decisions and no one that I know takes it personally. These boats are nearly the same, except for their dates of construction.

The M/V *Southport* weighs in at 424 gross tons. It is 180 feet long and 44 feet wide. It has a draft of 6 feet. It is painted in Duke University colors. The M/V *Fort Fisher* weighs in at 374 gross tons. It is the same size, but painted in the UNC-Wilmington colors. These boats belong to the River Class, which are the medium size boats. A slightly smaller boat is the Hatteras Class, with the largest boats being the Sound Class. The large ones can carry about 50 vehicles, and measure about 220 feet long and 50 feet wide. Their weights run around 770 gross tons.

The *Southport* and the *Fort Fisher* share the following characteristics. Their power comes from two Caterpillar diesel engines, mounted facing each other at about mid-ship below deck. They each are rated at about 500 horsepower. The drive shaft from each engine is connected to a Voith-Schneider drive box that spins the turntable below the hull and rotates the four blades of the drive mechanism. These blades change pitch according to the direction the helmsman wishes to go. This works very much like the drives of a helicopter, except the blades are only about

3.5 feet long and they hang down. When turning, they appear to work like beater blades on a kitchen mixer. What the Voith-Schneider drives give us is remarkable. The steering is precise and the thrust is phenomenal. The thrust vectoring provides great response, which eliminates the lag time found in rudder controlled, fixed prop drives. The whole drive is relatively compact and eliminates the forward-neutral-reverse shifting found in standard propeller driven boats.

These boats are referred to as double-enders. We do not have to turn around after loading vehicles. The bottom is shaped to accommodate this. In fact, at 100 percent power, we can change direction of travel 180 degrees without moving the throttle, all in the length of the boat. We can spin the boat completely around without tilting more than a few degrees. Just don't expect to reach break-neck speeds!

Each ferry has a small outboard powered rescue boat that can be lowered should someone go overboard, or assistance in a rescue becomes necessary. There are multiple inflatable life rafts, and life vests for everyone. Most of the safety equipment is required, and inspected by the Coast Guard regularly. In fact, the Coast Guard also has a required maintenance schedule for all boats, and full inspections scheduled for the hull and boat integrity. So rest assured, your safety is being looked after.

top: Captain Marybeth Ray at the helm
above: The view from dock
right: Looking towards Sunny Point from aboard the M/V *Southport*

Chapter 3

Safety, Safety, Safety

One of the main aspects of a deckhand's job is to load and unload the cars and passengers on the ferry. Although it may seem to be simple and quick work, there is more to it than pointing at a lane for the driver to get into. We try to load as many as possible, as quickly as possible. Preplanning is essential. Some vehicles just don't fit in certain spots. We always try to accommodate the handicapped passengers, and buses or vans with large doors. Oversized vehicles always present an opportunity to think ahead and use our experience. Certain spots on the ferry's deck, and walls, must remain accessible per Coast Guard (USCG) regulations. Chances are that most drivers of the vehicles will not be aware of this, so it is our job to make this happen in the middle of chaos, in all weather.

I want to share with you an observation on my part. I can't statistically prove this, but it is just my feeling. You should know first that I don't hide easily. I am 6'7" tall, and 285 pounds. I have pure white, not platinum blond, hair. I'm old by most standards. I have observed that the most difficult drivers to get cooperation from look just like me - old white guys! For some reason this group does not want to take directions from anyone. I can point, wave my arms, shout, and they often refuse to listen. I think it is simply the attitude that they know what they're doing and you can't tell them where to park their car on this boat! It seems to me that most other drivers outside of this small group are more than happy to accept help navigating this new endeavor. Sorry...old white guys, but women drivers are far more eager to receive, and accept help.

I am always amazed at the people that will pull on the ferry, park their car, and immediately jump out. Yes, right in front of the cars behind them or in the next lane. I am talking about adults, not children. We have to tell every single carload to stay in the vehicle until the Captain blows the horn for departure. I suppose it is eagerness to see over the side and get the full experience as quickly as possible. People just don't see the danger. So please, if you can't follow the rules of safety, please make sure you are a registered organ donor. Stupid hurts!

Another title for this chapter could be "Live to Tell the Story". It may not look like it, but every ferry crew member works hard to load the boat and put every vehicle in the safest position possible. It is not random, free range parking. We don't want to see your paint scratched or your legs cut and bruised from an oversized trailer hitch. If you are half as concerned about your safety as we are, you'll be fine. Still, we witness people on an almost daily basis put themselves and their family members at risk. Although these ferries are large and heavy, they can still pitch and bounce occasionally. The side rails, and Daddy's shoulders, are not safe places for children to sit. We don't want anyone going overboard or falling on a steel deck. We try to watch everyone. No one wants to ruin a statistically safe ferry ride with an injury of any type.

When I was 16 years old, I pulled a small child that I didn't know, off the bottom of the Albemarle Sound. You will notice that I didn't use the terminology "rescued". I handed his body to his screaming mother, as the group of searchers looked on at this horrible moment. He had been under for 45 minutes. That moment left a scar on my 16 year old heart. In January of 2010, my 25 year old son, Travis, passed away after a car wreck left him brain dead. A parent cannot erase the memory of a child being hauled in to the operating room for organ harvesting. Although there was a 40 year span between these events, they both changed me forever. Life is fragile and it can be taken in an instant. This small story that I've shared with you is very personal, and has but one purpose for you as a ferry passenger. That purpose is to help you understand, and hopefully forgive us, for being so passionate about the safety of you and your family while on our boats. To my knowledge, nothing of this degree has ever occurred on our ferries. As I have said, statistically the ferry is a safe place. Yet, we do everything possible to make sure anything this intense does not occur. So let's have fun!

The USCG regulates safety aboard all ferries. We do all the required safety drills and then some. Each ferry has all the safety gear required by the USCG. We are ready, should we need to use it. Please help us to never have to. And now I am speaking for myself from my own little soapbox, so forgive me a bit. For all of you that live in constant fear of other humans, as of now, your second amendment rights are firmly in place while on our ferries. If you feel you must, strap on your weapons and load up the ammo. As long as you carry per North Carolina laws, you can pack heat! Just do us all one small favor. Should you feel the need to use your weapon, PLEASE HIT YOUR TARGET! If you miss on a steel boat, the bullet should stop ricocheting in a week to ten days, unless it lodges in the soft tissue of an innocent child. So now I beg you from my own personal little soapbox, unless you are about to wet yourself with fear, please lock you weapon in the trunk or glove box. I learned a long time ago about mortality and how I am not bulletproof, even after many shots of tequila. Let us not argue personal rights here. There is a time and place for everything, and besides that, I like guns. It is just that on the boat, the dangers outweigh the benefits. This is meant to be a fun read, and not a political rant. So, let us move on.

Chapter 4

The Weather

My first days on the boat were perfect. Fall of the year here is wonderful, with the exception of the occasional hurricane. Unlike tornadoes and water spouts, hurricanes don't arrive unannounced.

When I expressed my concern about cold winter days coming, the younger guys told me that summer months with stagnate heat from the sun and car engines shutting down for the crossing was the real killer. I found this very true during my first year. The air temperature between the parked cars would easily reach the 135 degree mark. Once we get away from the ramp and in the river channel, a little breeze most often helped to bring the temperature down to a bearable level.

The weather will at times lend itself to passengers wanting to sit in their cars with the engine running for cool air or heat. You cannot have car engines running while the ferry is underway per USCG regulations. Most people understand when this is explained to them. However there are always the few that feel you are infringing on their rights. They don't think about the carbon monoxide blowing into the cars around them. Then there is always the possibility of a fire aboard caused by an overheated engine. If everyone would stop for just one drum beat and consider other people's health, safety, and quality of life before they proceed to meet their own desires, the whole world would be so much better. Alright, sorry, time to refocus.

Chapter 5

Location, Location, Location

During the winter season we must run several crossings a day in the dark. As Jimmy Buffett sang about, there is nothing like "Stars on the Water". The lights and the real stars overhead will make anyone smile and feel small. Then there is God's yellow moon rising full in the east over the ocean and the thin southern tip of New Hanover County that stretches toward Bald Head Island. As the sun slowly sinks over the Cape Fear River's western shore, that is Brunswick County, the glorious colors provide a beautiful photo opportunity.

During the thirty minute crossing of the Cape Fear River, you will cover five miles of water that is full of history and currently alive with present importance. Traveling south from Fort Fisher landing and looking at the western shoreline of the river, you will see Sunny Point Military Ocean Terminal. I tell people that if the US military owns it and it goes BOOM, it gets shipped out of there. The ships going in and out of there are very well protected by armed escorts from the USCG. If you are ever in a private boat near here, DO NOT ATTEMPT to approach the docks at Sunny Point. They will introduce themselves to you and delay your fun boating day.

Just south of Sunny Point is Duke Energy's Brunswick Nuclear Plant. It is a twin unit, boiling water reactor complex originally built by Carolina Power and Light. As the ferry approaches the Southport landing ramp and terminal, you will see a rather long pier extending to the edge of the river channel. This supports a pipeline that leads to the Archer-

Daniels-Midland (ADM) citric acid plant. Tanker ships off-load beet molasses from Poland and Central America using this pipeline. This is the raw product used for the production of citric acid.

As you drive off the ferry and leave our terminal area, you will see the Deep Point Harbor entrance that is the passage to Bald Head Island. The island is accessible by passenger ferry and private boats. No passenger cars are allowed on Bald Head Island. If this is not your destination, you will follow the signs and very quickly find yourself in beautiful South-port. You could simply drive around the town and enjoy the views and architecture of what was once a small fishing village at the entrance of the Cape Fear River. Other options include guided tours, either by walk-ing, riding on golf carts, or a tour trolley. One option that a lot of people choose, is to walk the waterfront and the downtown area on a self-guided tour at your own pace. The town is full of history, from the pirates of the 1700's, to the busy film industry work of the last thirty years. One of our ferry boats usually ends up in every movie filmed here. If they don't actually film on board, they will use shots of the ferry underway during opening scenes.

Immediately upon leaving the ramp at the Southport landing, you will see a small cone-shaped structure on the ADM property next to the pier. It is the Prices Creek Lighthouse from the early 1800's. ADM does a wonderful job preserving this piece of history. It was one of the origi-nal five river lighthouses used by ships to navigate the Cape Fear River to Wilmington. This is the only one left standing. As you cruise north up the river from the Southport landing, you will see Bald Head Island and Oak Island to the south. The Oak Island Lighthouse will be flashing its signature four flashes. There is no light currently in the Bald Head Lighthouse. It was repaired and freshened up in 2016-17. So this gives everyone the opportunity to see three lighthouses from one spot.

Looking east, towards the Atlantic, you will see a strip of land that connects southern New Hanover County to Brunswick County and Bald Head. Several small inlets originally cut this strip causing constant shoaling in the river channel. The US Army Corp of Engineers began a project in 1871 that lasted until 1891 that created a concrete wall along the river side of the strip. This wall is about four miles long and blocks all water flow to and from the ocean into the river, greatly reducing the shoaling problems. The wall itself is built much like a beaver dam. It uses cypress tree trunks buried in the bottom and covered with limestone boulders and cement. The top of this dam is barely visible now at high tide. Perhaps this has something to do with rising ocean levels. Depends on who you ask! The son of the engineer that led this project was the engineer in charge of building the retaining wall in the Potomac River for the Lincoln Memorial. That is why the two walls that are 500 miles apart look alike.

As you leave the Fort Fisher landing and head north on US 421, you will see the entrance to the North Carolina Aquarium at Fort Fisher. It draws a steady crowd all year. It is definitely a "must see" in this area. It even has a petting pool, and every year has a special added attraction. It is educational and fun. Consider it a gift to your child and an honest treat for any adult. The next thing you'll encounter going north is the Fort Fisher Civil War site. On the east side of the road is one of the most beautiful stands of Live Oaks that exist in the south today. If you continue traveling north up US 421, you will understand why Carolina Beach, Wilmington, and Wrightsville Beach, have one of the hottest real estate markets in North Carolina.

All of this, and the daily commuter traffic, keeps us busy year round. The snowbird river boat traffic in the fall and spring, along with the ships using the Wilmington Ports, provide for changing scenery. The commuters become important pieces in the fabric of this job. They are friends that sometime become like family. If one of us is missing for more than

top: Container cranes at Sunny Point Military Ocean Terminal
above: view of the river from inside passenger lounge
right: Remaining base of Price's Creek Lighthouse

one day, they will ask the crew about us. They help us to keep an eye out for anything out of the ordinary.

We watch the wildlife daily. We see baby dolphins grow and depart their briny river birthplace. We see herds of deer, and stealthy alligators, along the banks near the Southport landing. To see this all is truly a gift.

below: the view south, towards the Oak Island lighthouse
bottom: an oceangoing ship

top: birds on old dredge spoil island that is now a federally protected breeding ground
middle: 8' alligator at Southport landing
bottom: ADM pier and dock for off loading beet molasses

Chapter 6

Why Everyone Should Ride a Ferry

I really feel that you should ride a ferry, be it auto or passenger somewhere as close to home as possible. With my life's experiences, I say make a point to ride a North Carolina ferry on one of the routes along our coast.

Permit me to clear up something now. I'm not the guy that will argue with you that North Carolina is the greatest state in the union. It has been good for me. The weather is mostly wonderful. The people are usually helpful and friendly. The topography is varied, along with the seasons. Neither is extreme. But all things are based on your perspective. I love other states for what they also offer. I've just always been happier to live here, and visit there. I'm also refusing to discuss the political slants that each of us must consider when you move the whole family or just yourself to a new state. I realize it is all personal, but North Carolina has seen a huge influx of new residents in the recent years. I like to think that our new North Carolinians are bringing fresh eyes and new ideas, on how to make this state even better.

As I age, I try to stay positive. It depresses me that our society has become more interested in expressing what is wrong with everything. Let's find out what is good, and double down on it! So it is time to step down off the soapbox again. Let's get back to why everyone should ride a ferry.

Today, very few people travel by water. So a ferry trip will be a different experience that will provide a new perspective. The scenery is different from the billboards of the roadways. Where else can you travel and bring your car like a piece of carry-on luggage? How convenient. On calm days, you get a sense of tranquility that you can't get just anywhere. During bad weather, you can get a taste of how unforgiving Mother Nature can be.

With just a little imagination, you can scan the shoreline and horizon realizing that the pirates Stede Bonnet, Edward Teach (a.k.a. Blackbeard), and others used this very same vantage point. The Cape Fear River was explored by the Italian explorer Giovanni de Verrazzano in 1524 on a mission from the King of Spain. He also sailed the Chesapeake Bay and most famously, the Hudson River in New York. If you are ever around the New York City area and spot the Verrazzano Narrows Bridge, remember that he found the Cape Fear River first.

This stretch of the Cape Fear River, from the Orange Street docks in Wilmington, south to the Atlantic Ocean, was used as the only water-borne section of the now famous "Underground Railroad". From here, smuggled slaves seeking freedom traveled to the Caribbean Islands aboard rum runners and spice boats. The first and the main boat to be used for this endeavor was said to have been the "Sally Anne", which was named after the Captain's mother, Sally Anne Swain. The Swains were Quakers from Wales originally. This gave them reason to be part of this, since slavery was against Quaker belief. Captain Swain had paid for the freedom of two slaves that were brothers and promptly put them aboard as deckhands. He had also bought freedom for their wives, which stayed ashore to help as midwives. This was the perfect cover, should anyone see a black man aboard the Sally Anne as she sailed in and out of Wilmington. No one ever questioned if any others were aboard. My Mother, Hester Anne, was a Carolina Swain before marrying my Dad. When I found the connection in my family history, I smiled as many questions became clear to me about beliefs that my Grandad had handed down to me. Now I knew why his farm in Creswell, NC had three families living in three homes that never paid a penny for rent. The belief and brotherhood was a family tradition that I became proud of. Now, look who's a deckhand!

If you are traveling on the ferry alone, relish the quiet time for introspective thought, and let your imagination run wild. If you have a loving partner with you, then the salt air and water will enrich the romance. When you find yourself on the ferry with young kids, seize the wonderful opportunity to plant seeds of wisdom that will encourage them to learn more. Spark their imagination with "What ifs" and "glimpses into the future". Kids get bored just hearing about the past. Help them envision the possibilities of the coming years.

Don't let them only see what is on the water. Encourage them to question what is "in" the water. Get them to think about how much they can't see. All the various life forms that live in the water make up part of what they can consider. Help them to think about unfound artifacts from pirate days and lost items from all over the world that have fallen from, or have been tossed from foreign ships making passage to the port docks in Wilmington. The young child that you encourage to think today, may very well turn out to be the thirty year old that solves the world's environmental, engineering, or biological problems in the future. You have the gift to plant those seeds.

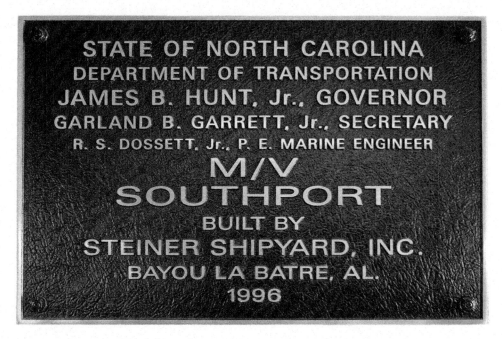

STATE OF NORTH CAROLINA
DEPARTMENT OF TRANSPORTATION
JAMES B. HUNT, Jr., GOVERNOR
GARLAND B. GARRETT, Jr., SECRETARY
R. S. DOSSETT, Jr., P. E. MARINE ENGINEER
M/V
SOUTHPORT
BUILT BY
STEINER SHIPYARD, INC.
BAYOU LA BATRE, AL.
1996

Chapter 7

Jack's Advice

My Dad, Jack Modlin, did not have a Ph.D., Master's Degree, nor a diploma of any type. He did have an Honorable Discharge from the US Army after Korea, a love of God, family, and all people. One of his pieces of advice that I cherish so dearly to this day, is a must for me to share with you now. He said, "Take every opportunity to sit down at a table and share a meal with somebody that doesn't look like you." His theory was that you may, or may not, learn to like a new dish, but you will definitely learn about that person's path through life. Bottom line is, everyone will be better for the time at that table. Dad really enjoyed going to the dirt track races in Wilson, NC on the occasional Saturday night. One time on the way home after a race we came upon a large gathering in a field beside the road. The Highway Patrol and Sheriff's Department were there directing traffic safely by the event. Dad pulled to the shoulder with Mom and my 11 year old self in the car. With the windows down on a hot summer night, we could hear the rant from the loudspeakers. We sat without uttering a word to each other for about ten minutes. I had never heard such ugly language and hate coming from anyone in my life. Then they cheered and set a cross on fire. Mom told Dad that we needed to go. That is when I asked Dad why he stopped to hear a KKK rally. He told me in the most sincere tone that I had ever heard my Dad speak, "I stopped for you to hear it". He told me that he wanted to be with me when I heard something like that for the first and hopefully last time. He told me that should I find myself somewhere in the future when that sort of hate was being preached, as if it were God's word, then I would remember this night, recognize the evil, and remove myself from it as quickly as possible. Thank you Dad! Those parental teachings enable me to speak without fear to everyone that comes onto our ferry. It makes me want to get to know you, and make your trip fun and memorable. Mom and Dad loved to travel and show their little boy everything they could. Most parents are that way. Our travels were limited to places that we could afford.

Most trips were day trips around the state. Growing up in northeastern North Carolina resulted in the Ferry System being a major part of my life. Just to get from home, in Martin County, to Nags Head, required two ferry crossings in those years. Both were part of US 64, with one crossing at Alligator River, and the other one across Roanoke Sound, just prior to Roanoke Island and Manteo.

If your destination was Ocracoke Island, two more crossings were required. NC 12 that runs down the Outer Banks had a ferry at Oregon Inlet, providing access to Hatteras Island, and another between Hatteras and Ocracoke Island. The entire trip resulted in a seven to eight hour journey. Bridges are now in place across the Alligator River, Roanoke Sound, and Oregon Inlet. Ocracoke is serviced by ferries from three directions. Hatteras Island, Swan Quarter, and Cedar Island terminals, all make runs to Ocracoke Island. Swan Quarter and Cedar Island use the Silver Lake landing at the south end, while the Hatteras to Ocracoke lands at the north end of the island.

My childhood vacations were trips to different places and experiences that didn't cost over a few week's salary for my Dad. For a paper mill employee, that could be limiting. The ferries provided us with a family boating experience. I think it gave birth to my love for the water and boating.

Every summer, Dad, Mom, and I, would load up the car and head to New Jersey to spend a week with my Uncle John and Aunt Carol Modlin. This trip always guaranteed two things, a Yankees game and a ferry ride across the Chesapeake Bay from Norfolk, Virginia to the Del-Mar-Va peninsula. It was a two hour crossing that covered 22 miles of open water. I never slept one minute on this portion of the trip. I would usually keep up with every mile covered on the entire trip, using a map.

I regrettably never rode the Staten Island Ferry while in the New York area. However, as a thirteen year old, we did take the New York Circle Tour, which took you by passenger ferry around Manhattan Island. What an educational experience for a kid from the south. Thank you Mom, Dad, Aunt Carol, and Uncle John. For a kid that grew up in the tobacco fields of northeastern North Carolina, I was able to tool around New York without fear of getting lost. I will not say that fear didn't come into play at times. After all, this was New York City in the 60's and 70's. I always loved the city for what it gave to me.

This is one of the key reasons that I get so much pleasure from seeing families interacting on the ferry, here on the Cape Fear. When I see parents answering questions from their kids, I know that seed I spoke of earlier is being planted. A desire to learn more about this rock called Earth may be getting born at that very minute. My pet peeve, the smart phone, is not being stared at in a zombie state. It is far more important not to miss this moment with your family, than it is to keep up with the Kardashians. I sincerely want to believe that kids are able to interpret this attention from Mom and Dad as love. They aren't overhearing their parents complain about life or politics. Chances are that they will remember this, just like I did. If you are talking to your kids, maybe the wrong people will not get a chance to.

Chapter 8

Visitors from Switzerland

While loading the ferry on the Fort Fisher side one day, we saw a fascinating motor home come aboard. The tag on the front bumper was a Swiss plate. As we began our crossing, I just had to find out all I could about this vehicle. The couple and car were from Switzerland. They had it custom built in Germany, and the interior handcrafted in Switzerland. This motor home looked as if it could take on any terrain. It was astoundingly functional and well designed. The couple appeared to be in their late fifties or early sixties. They had the motor home shipped to the United States after its construction. They planned to use this as their American vacation home. They had three months of "holiday", every year. So each year they come to the US and tour around the country. On this wonderful day, they had arrived at my coordinates.

They shared with me what they had seen and what amazed them the most. During that encounter I was almost brought to tears with my laughter at their observations. They were the most happy and positive people that I had seen in a long time. He told me how we should cherish the life and the scenery that we have in this country. This is coming from someone that has the Alps outside their window at home. They went on and on about how much they loved touring the US and meeting people.

As they were about to depart at the Southport landing, they waved goodbye and continued their journey. I sincerely hope that they are doing well and staying happy. They certainly "gifted" me that day with their attitude of appreciation and hope for our country.

Chapter 9

Bumper Stickers

It seems like everyone has something on their mind that they want to throw out to everyone else. With the abundance on social media available, one would think that bumper stickers would have become too old school for most people, yet it remains an outlet for us as humans to share our level of intelligence and passions. Using your car may not be the most financially wise decision, but don't let common sense get in the way.

Honestly, the crew reads them all, in hope of getting a laugh. However, some just bring pain. Once, I was compelled to share my wisdom with a young millennial that proudly displayed a sticker in his back window that used the F-word. It said; "F*** your stick family", with the F-word was spelled out. I explained that it didn't matter if it was intended to be funny, the father in the SUV behind him at that very moment was having to explain the F-word to his six year old daughter. I told him that one day maybe he would understand by having to do the same thing that father was doing. Just think about the possible effects that your decisions may have on others. Have I said that already?

Here is a hot topic issue that I'm not afraid of. The display of the Confederate Battle Flag. I was born and raised in the south, yet I cannot fathom why so many on both sides of the issue are so passionate about it. I say "both sides" as if there are only two ways to look at this. I thought so at one time in my life, but age and education taught me to have a new perspective that was far less extreme. I'll just ask you to try it and see if you feel happier.

I've heard the whole "Heritage not Hate" viewpoint. That's nice, but just because you were born in the south, or even if you had ancestors that died in that horrible conflict, it doesn't force you to tie your entire heritage to the 1860's. Can't you find anything more positive that defines you? Someone in your family must have lived through something else. Someone must have done something positive for mankind. Make the Civil War what it is, history. Stop beating the dead dog. It was ugly and slavery was wrong. Enough already. Yes, many civilizations practiced slavery, but take note that it no longer legally exists.

The other extreme is that the flag and the leaders of the south were all evil, and any recognition or memory of their existence should be erased. That is simply not true. The best reason for remembering history and its details, is the same reason for studying it. If we don't learn history, we are doomed to repeat it. When I saw a bumper sticker on a van that had the rebel flag on it, and it read "I still pledge my life and allegiance to this flag", my heart nearly stopped. I didn't have to look inside to know what kind of people owned it. We need to spend more time looking forward to unity and figure out how to lessen the divisiveness.

One day I paused to notice the back window of an SUV that had been covered along the edges of the glass in small Confederate Battle Flags. They were about 2 inches by 3 inches. There must have been sixty or more flags very neatly placed. The rear of the SUV was otherwise vacant of anything derogatory. From behind me, the owner of the SUV asked me what I thought of his art work. Very truthfully, I told him that it showed great skill and was very tastefully done. Instead of saying thank you, he went on to angrily state that he had as much right to fly his flag as the car next to him had the right to fly their flag. I looked over and saw the flag of Great Britain on a plate bolted to the front bumper. I stepped to the rear of the car to see the North Carolina license tag. I told him that he was right, it appeared that someone from North Carolina had a British heritage. I wanted so badly to ask him if he was aware that Great

Britain was still a country. Although he called the Confederate Flag "his" flag, I'm quite sure the American flag is his current flag. After leaving the gentleman feeling vindicated, I thought of how troubling this was to me. He had his point of view, and I had mine. I had always tried to act and live in a manner that would dispel misconceptions that southern white men are stupid and small minded. He really aligned his love and heritage to a flag that only flew during a few years of the Civil War, to that of a country that still exist after all these years.

This gets me back to my suggestion. We have got to let it go. Let the teenage southern boys fly their battle flags from the beds of jacked up pick-up trucks. They will grow up and hopefully find something worthwhile and currently relevant to become passionate about. I really didn't have a clue at that age either. This area is rich in Civil War history and the southern plantation life of that period. While you are here, visit the forts, settlements, and sites. Add to your knowledge and take a minute to think of where we have been in this country. It will make us wiser as we move forward. Try your best to develop some empathy for the less fortunate of that historical period. I am talking about the period in time and the war that pitted family members against one another, and humans that were only counted as three-fifths of a person.

If I notice a bumper sticker or license tag that denotes organ donation, Purple Heart recipient, or anything worthy such as medical professional, I will offer up a sincere "Thank you". This is a job where you get to show your appreciation of others. There are tons of mean spirited or ugly bumper stickers, especially during election seasons. I just ignore them. On some narcissistic level in some damaged mind, this must make some people feel superior. I have taken the attitude that they are helping me and everyone else save time on forming an opinion by being up front about who they really are.

Chapter 10

Unpleasant Incidents

Every now and then, a boat crew will find itself in a situation that just isn't normal, and may be out of our area of expertise. We train for things that you would expect to go wrong on a boat, such as fire, man overboard, oil spills, bomb threats, and terrorist activities. But leave it to humans to give us an occasional challenge. Sometimes it is more "Saturday Night Live" than anything else, yet sometimes we have to get serious and improvise.

On this given day, there was a couple that had engaged in a domestic dispute in a not so domestic environment. They walked on as passengers without drawing attention to their difficulties. We didn't have a clue what was transpiring until shore security called our Captain and told her that someone had reported a man being abusive to a woman. We quickly spotted them after leaving the dock. We spent the entire thirty minute crossing successfully keeping them apart by isolating her and having four crew members constantly surveil him. As he paced around the deck in search of her, a crew member would occasionally confront him, and ask him if we could help. He would tell his story that his girlfriend had wandered off and he was looking for her. We would tell him that she had to be on the boat and he would find her when we docked. That helped to slow down his search, and give our Captain time to call Fort Fisher terminal for help to assist her safety. Once on the other side, security called a ride service for her, and called the cops on him. Problem, at least our part, was over. I'm sure it wasn't for her, but what else could we do? This is where the importance of a good level headed crew, with a Captain that thinks before acting, is so crucial. When things that could potentially go bad, turn out this good, then you have to stop and count your blessings.

On the very next day in a most bizarre twist, on the very same last run of the day, we had our next trial by fire so to speak. Somehow, an impaired driver made it past security by faking sobriety long enough to start down the loading ramp without the slightest problem. As she came down the ramp, our Ship's Mate Coby Benson noticed her veering to the railing and then slump over. The lady's daughter grabbed the wheel to avoid hitting the guardrail and applied the brakes. We guessed the daughter to be in her early teens. We got the car parked on the ferry and chocked in place so we could get underway. Coby gave the car keys to the Captain. Our Captain Marybeth Ray tried to get the lady to respond to no avail. The NC Highway Patrol was contacted and showed up at the Fort Fisher landing in time to get the car off of the ferry so we could get back and complete the final run for the day.

above: Captain Marybeth Ray at the helm
right: M/V *Southport* pulling in at Ft. Fisher landing

Chapter 11

Sleeping Commuters

We have a regular group of commuters that traverse the Cape Fear River to get to their jobs. The numbers seem fairly balanced from both sides. These people become familiar to us and we count on them to help us make the loading and unloading go smoothly. Some come up to the passenger lounge on a regular basis and share stories with us. They become our "work family", and seem to honestly care about our well- being. At the holidays, they will sometimes share cards and sincere thanks. It makes all of us feel cherished and essential. What do you know? We're not invisible!

The commuters learn to use their time wisely. Some read, some make phone calls, tweet, text, or just rub the screens of their smart phones. Some sleep, hoping to wake up when we pull under the ramp and bump the pilings. If the weather and temperature permits, they will curl up with the windows up. Many bring blankets for the colder months. Occasionally, with embarrassing results, a few miss the wake up bump at the ramp. The drone of the diesel engines, and the sounds of sea gulls, all contribute to the perfect storm for nap-time. We most often wake them up with a tapping on the glass or hood. However, a few reach REM sleep and require a little more. If they are blocking the traffic, which is usually the case, they get the unfriendly glare of the other passengers. We just smile, because we understand.

On one trip, a lady that was alone had fallen asleep during the crossing. We had no clue that she had just visited the dentist office and had a

little leftover residual help at relaxation. Upon awakening, she fumbled to get her car started and in gear. She then took off, IN REVERSE. Our Mate, Coby Benson, charged her frantically and managed to get her stopped before she backed into the cargo safety netting at the rear of the boat. After a few moments of head clearing, she proceeded in the correct direction and departed without further difficulties.

Chapter 12

Lost Jewelry

Once in a while, we will find a piece of costume jewelry that was lost. I've not seen anyone find anything of serious value. But let this tale be a warning to you about lost things. Several smart phones and pairs of glasses have been found and most all make their way back to their owners.

Years ago, if you found an earring that was really nice, you had found something of value. But life, and people's desires have changed. Before you pick it up, think about where, as in point of origin, it may have come from.

This tale will be told as delicately as possible in consideration for whomever may read it. Immediately after leaving the Fort Fisher ramp, the four occupants of a small car, exited the car and headed up the stairs to the passenger lounge area. Three young ladies and one young man, all around twenty years old. After completing my security walk, I proceeded up the stairs to the passenger lounge myself. That is where I found the aforementioned four young people gathered. Two of the young ladies were seated facing the rear of the lounge, with the young man on the seat in front of them also facing rearward. Directly in front of him stood the other young lady facing him. He was leaning forward as if he were studying a non-existent belt buckle. At this point, as strange as it appeared, I did not stare. As I took my seat, that also faced rearward, behind the first two young ladies, I saw but failed to accept what was going on. She had lifted her skirt and removed whatever else she may have had on, and was patiently waiting for him to re-attach her jewelry, that was piercing her most private of areas. I quickly removed myself from this equation. I cannot verify that the re-attachment was a success.

After getting over the initial shock of seeing this fine example of friends helping friends, I started questioning my current life's perspective. When did I get this old? Or maybe the question should be; when did boy-girl relationships evolve into this area? Who knows? What are friends for? A hundred years ago, when I was twenty years old, most guys didn't even know where this small pinnacle of pleasure was. Now, this guy finds a small hole through it to hang jewelry. Has mankind really come this far. Or was this young man just as clueless, and merely doing as she directed him? I am pretty sure that the young lady was well aware of what she had accomplished, and most appreciative of his assistance. But an unanswered and most obvious fact was their total lack of caring that I, and anyone else there, could witness this.

above: NC Ferry System logo
right: ramp controls at Ft. Fisher landing

Chapter 13

Victoria

This is a tale where I must use invented names for the individuals, in order to tell the story just as it occurred. So the passenger's name and the name of the other ferry employee is totally made up by me. But I was there, and every fact is true. I feel the tale is the important part. Revealing the true identities is not.

A lady walked into the passenger lounge one beautifully clear and warm October Saturday, on our next to last run. She struck up a conversation with the other deckhand and myself, about creeks to fish in off the river. She sat down across the table from Ben, our other deckhand that day. Ben was a pool employee, and standing in for someone else. Ben was a few years older than me, and fancied himself quite the lady's man. I had threatened to nickname him Pepe, after Pepe La Pew in the cartoon. She told us her name and the various places she had lived in the area. She joked about drinking all afternoon in Carolina Beach, or at least we thought she was joking. When I commented to her that she looked familiar, she laughed and told me that we had met many years and a lifetime ago. This got the memory wheels turning, but I just could not place her, or the name. She got touchy-feely with Ben, in a nice lady like way. Only the hand and forearm were part of this game. Ben obviously appreciated her friendly touch.

It came time for passengers to get back in their cars and for us to prepare to unload. Victoria gave Ben a goodbye hug, shook my hand and smiled. As the cars drove off the ferry, Victoria pulled from the lane we call the tunnel, which is under the superstructure. Somehow, she didn't see the last steel support column and sideswiped it with her car. It caved in the driver door a little, and raised the front left wheel off the deck. It had done no visible damage to the column, except for scratching the paint. She leaned out of the driver's door window and surveyed the damages to her car. She looked at Ben and I, smiled and said, "It'll buff out" and drove off.

As they say; "Curiosity killed the cat, but the cat died happy". I had to know why she told me what she did, and why my memory alarm was ringing. So when I got home, I got on the computer and went to a popular general locater website. I typed in Victoria and her last name. After looking at several Victorias, I was coming up blank. So I took and even wider pool to pull from, using Vickie and Vicky. Still nothing in the right area and age. So I made it simple and just used "V" and the last name. Of course, now I was looking at hundreds of combination using Victoria, Vickie, Vicky, which I had previously found. Only this time it included Victor, Vick, and Vic with the same last name.

BOOM! There it was. Shame on me, for not thinking of all possibilities in this current world. There was Victor with the same surname as Victoria. Every previous address matched, Victor's time in Long Beach matched when I was single and hitting the bars on the island. Now I remember Vick, as everyone called him. According to what I found, Vick decided to become Victoria around 2005. I remember Vick as a nice guy that treated people well. I had once asked him out of deep sincerity, if he thought he might have a drinking problem. He told me that he considered it a solution. I laughed because he never caused anyone a problem, except maybe himself. He never got falling down drunk. He was just always drinking gently, as I refer to it. Now, Victoria seems to be a nice lady, and treats everyone well, even though she is quite the drinker. Most importantly, she seemed truly happy that October day, so all's well, that ends well. The guy I knew as Vick had found the woman of his dreams. It was Victoria. I was happy for him.

The next day, Ben was with us again on the boat. I kept quiet about Victoria until Ben brought her up. He thought she was really interesting and fairly nice looking. He said that there just seemed to be a rough edge to her that he couldn't figure out. I laughed and told him that all of us have rough edges as we age. He agreed and stated that it didn't matter, she seemed genuinely good and would probably be fun to hang out with. That is when I told Ben that he was correct. She used to be that way when I knew her. Ben began to beg me to tell him what I had remembered about her. He remembered that she told me that I would figure it out later. I began telling Ben what I had found about Victoria. I told him that what I remembered was Vick. After telling him the whole story, Ben made me promise not to tell anyone that he held her hand that long. So if you are reading this "Ben", I kept my promise. Yes, I told the story, but not the names and dates. The ferry crews will not know who "Ben" really is. So you're safe. Let's hope that Victoria stays safe also.

below: passenger lounge

Chapter 14

Students By The Bus load

On a fairly regular basis, we have bus loads of school students that use the ferries. They come from all over, but for the most part, North Carolina. Their destination usually involves Fort Fisher and the NC Aquarium. I'm truly glad to see this field trip option still exist with all the politicians trying to tell us how to educate kids with less and less money.

It is interesting to see the focus and approach that various age groups have when given the gift of a field trip. Honestly, as crew members, we dread to see the buses coming. It seldom means a relaxing ride, and often leads to the severe biting of one's tongue. When 35 or so kids rush into the passenger lounge and fight over eight electrical outlets to charge their devices on, screams fill our heads. At times, in the middle of all this, God will send us a gift.

On this day, it was my turn to get the "gift". I was sitting at a table in the lounge, going over some charts when I heard a very timid and perfect voice say, "Excuse me sir". I looked up to see what I guessed to be, a 10 year old boy. Thinking he wanted an electrical plug or the location of the rest room, I said "Yes, how can I help you young man? With a calm, and well thought out question, he asked, "What type of propulsion does this ship use?"

I was blown away. I sat straight up and asked him to have a seat while I explained it to him and drew some rough sketches for him. I wrote down some terms and told him what to look up on the computer, when he got home. My heart was filled with joy. I couldn't wait to get home and tell my wife. He was with a group of 10 to 12 year olds from about sixty miles inland. With a little luck and guidance, this ten year old kid could turn out to be one of Columbus County's most famous marine design engineers. We need to entice these kids to enjoy their lives and learn how to make this world better. This young black man already had that desire. Someone in his life loved him very much. That child made my day worth living. He was the day's gift to me.

below: the view astern towards Fort Fisher

Chapter 15

Levels
of Expectation

Some families plan ahead and pack a little picnic snack to share with the group during the crossing. It is just another way to make a memory, and I admire that. It is always interesting and somewhat of a sociological study to take note of how different parents organize the seemingly simple family evolution. Don't jump to any conclusions or pre-conceived ideas here. I think it is a very personality driven event, where there is no right or wrong way, in most cases.

Some people are totally anal-retentive about hygiene. This same group tends to push the obsessive-compulsive limits also on portions. If there are six people, they will all have equal numbers of nuts, candies, chips, and the like. Everyone will have the identical fruit drink. Every item will be individually wrapped. Little pre-wetted wipes and sanitizer will be available for all upon entering the top-of-the-line mini-van or SUV.

Then comes the group that I am more aligned with. This group practices the free range, open plate, free for all, bulk packaged items with every soft drink and sweet tea available. Pre-wetted wipes and sanitizer will still be available before entering the truck. What? I've got some dignity, and fears. See, I told you. No right or wrong. Get the troops fed and make a memory. This tale is just an example of the vast difference in attitudes, from people of different influences. This is where level of expectation comes into play.

A lady walked into the passenger lounge one day with four small children following her closely in single file. I can't say for certain, however using my power of deduction, I guessed her age to match mine closely, which in my mind made her the probable Grandma. Judging by the size and quality of jewelry, and the expensive handbag, I felt safe to assume that she was not financially suffering. They found a table across from where I was sitting, and proceeded to spread out their carefully planned snack items. The kids picked and bantered between each other as children do. The lady attempted to maintain complete control of the little gang of four. Although I was sitting directly across the aisle from them, less than four feet away, not once did she acknowledge my existence. Not a friendly "Hello" or smile. I just thought that maybe she was totally overwhelmed with Grandma duties. I would soon figure out, or at least assume, that the reason was because I was invisible to her due to my service level. I would only be seen, if I were needed for a task.

As we approached the Fort Fisher landing, I informed her that we would be unloading in about five minutes. For the first time, she looked me straight in the eye and in a most serious voice she makes the statement, "Someone cleans this up for us, don't they?" I am not an expert on the English language by no means. Sadly though, it is my only language, yet I was bewildered. With only eight words, (OK, one is a contraction) she had told me my place in society and her level of expectation. I answered her with more politeness than she deserved. "No ma'am, everyone cleans up after themselves." I then pointed out the trash receptacle, and went down to unload.

When I returned to the area, they had picked up their trash and put it in the can. I cleaned the table with sanitizer and prepped the area for our next passengers. I doubt seriously that I got a little smiley face on her trip review card. You have to try and forgive people like this. After all, slavery and indentured servitude was only one hundred and fifty years ago. It takes some people a little longer to adjust to big changes. PLEASE, don't take me seriously!

Less than two weeks passed, and two men with matching shirts on, from a tech company in Raleigh, entered the passenger lounge carrying several small coolers. They sat at the same table that the lady from the previous story had sat at with the children. Between the two men, they had enough snacks and finger food to feed a family of eight. They asked me immediately if it was alright to spread out the food on the table. Of course, was my reply to them. They asked me to come and join them for a snack. I kindly refused, telling them that I had just eaten lunch. For the entire crossing, they snacked and asked everyone that came by, if they would like to share with them. They both would smile at every passenger. I told them that we were about to come into the dock at Southport. I had to thank them for their generosity and willingness to share. One of the gentlemen was from North Carolina, and the other gentleman was a new American citizen of Egyptian birth. They actually asked me for a cloth to wipe off the table. I told them not to worry, that I would gladly do that before we loaded.

Of these two tales from different days, it is easy to tell which one displayed what should be the American way. I am a firm believer in pleasantly assimilating one's self to gain acceptance into a different culture, as long as that goes in the right direction. But I am truly happy when someone comes to our country and shows us how to be decent to other humans. We should be the ones setting that standard, but thank God it all works out. I think of when the term "Ugly American" was coined, and how it had nothing to do with physical attractiveness. We all need to strive to make the "Ugly American" extinct.

Chapter 16

Seriously Folks

There are, and there always will be opportunists without principals. Some people always look for the entity or the individual with the deepest pockets to gain their wealth in this litigious society. We occasionally have the passenger that will complain about a scratched fender or a broken mirror, when the entire side of the vehicle is dented and rusty from a wreck years earlier. They know how difficult it is for a Captain or terminal manager to call them out on their claims. Not because their claim may be reasonable, but simply because it is so hard to fathom why anyone would lie and endanger an employee's job over an incident that just may have no plausibility. This is just part of the "it is all about me" attitude of the last couple of decades.

One of the other things that we find ourselves asking the "Are you serious?" question to, is the things that passengers do once they are aboard the boat that goes against safety or USCG regulations. As you start down the ramp to board the ferry, you will see a plethora (bunches and bunches) of signs that tell you what to do and absolutely what not to do once aboard. Are you trying to tell me that you didn't read every one of them in the allotted three seconds as you passed by trying not to hit the guardrail? This is why we don't mind telling you once you are aboard. We understand, seriously folks! This is a new experience for many of you, so you are forgiven. Please don't argue with us when we reveal these rules and regulations to you. We didn't make them, we only enforce them. There is a lot of reasoning and logic behind most of them.

No smoking! The last place you want a fire is on a plane or a boat. It is hard to run away. Fire fighting capabilities are fairly good, but not the greatest. Even if it doesn't cause a fire aboard the boat, there is another problem. When one of the crew, or even the Captain spots smoke, guess what? We have to quickly verify that we do not have a fire aboard. Just hang on for thirty minutes and you can fire one up when you leave the boat.

The engines have to be off also. Again, fire is the main reason. One of the other reasons is you may run out of fuel. We have had people restart their car once we make our security pass, and then run out of fuel before they reach the other side. Trying to stay cool inside the car during the hot summer months was more important than looking at their gas gauge. Once on the other side, the crew members had to push the car off the boat and UP the ramp, in order to reload the ferry.

Modern technology has brought on another problem. Every auto turns into a charging outlet for all the new devices such phones, games, iPads, and the like. Within thirty minutes the vehicle's battery is dead, and we have another blockage in the unloading evolution. With the increased number of vehicles that have push button start, we have more and more drivers just get out of their vehicles and leave them running. At least the Mate or Captain can announce this over the loudspeaker system, and usually find the owner. Cars with the new electronic parking brakes seem to bewilder a lot of people. They push the button to apply the brake, but when they try to leave they realize that they have no clue how to disengage the parking brake. Honestly, we understand this a little bit. It seems that every car maker has a different method to disengage the brake. This does make me feel a little better about my inability to handle new technology at times.

right: USCG maintained channel marker in Cape Fear River

Chapter 17

Angels Come In All Sizes

There is a date associated with this tale. It occurred on January 23, 2017. It was a relatively cold, but clear day. Not too bad for this time of year on the water. I was sitting in the passenger lounge, speaking with a visitor to the area about something. A couple came by with the cutest of little girls walking behind them. She appeared to be seven or eight years old. She smiled and waved at me as she passed. That was enough to make me feel good about the day, but more would come. As her parents took a seat, and began talking to her about the birds, dolphins and sights on the river, she kept turning to check on me. No one other than the earlier mentioned gentleman visitor had approached me during the latter two thirds of the trip. I had been sitting there lost in my thoughts and struggles of the day. It was time to prepare to land and unload, so I went out and descended the steps to the main deck.

As the vehicles were leaving the boat, a full size, dark SUV stopped next to me and the man told me that his daughter had something for me. That is when I recognized him and his wife, as the couple in the lounge area with the little girl. The tinted glass of the rear door came down and the little girl stuck her head out and gave me a little yellow flower that she had fashioned from a rubber band. She said, "You look like you need a present today, sir. You seem down." I looked at her mother and told her that I really needed that and her daughter had perfect timing. Your daughter is truly my little angel for the day. I wanted to tell them why, but others were waiting to get off the ferry, so I had to let them go. I smiled at the young girl and thanked her. I told her that God had sent her to me that day, and to keep smiling at people.

That day, seven years earlier, my youngest son had been killed in a car wreck. I had been withdrawn and quiet all day. My heart and soul hurt with the memory. The crew knew what the situation was, so they had given me a break all day from the usual picking and joking that we do. That little angel saw something in me, and sensed the pain. In just a moment of time, she changed me that day. I was going to make it, largely because of her and the yellow rubber band flower. I sincerely hope that her parents read this, so they will understand why it meant so much to me. God bless them all.

These people that come into our lives at the strangest and most perfectly timed moments, are given the title "Angel" by me. Believe me please, I am not the person that constantly talks about religion and faith. I don't fall into prayer every time I feel a need for something. I feel that God is busy, and has a lot on the plate of life. I don't want to bother God with the small stuff. But I will say my thanks when a blessing is received. I look at an angel as any entity that helps us to feel better, or to do better. Sometimes it is just an opportunity.

This is a short tale about a person that became one of those "opportunities". We were about to make the turn into the channel on approach to Fort Fisher landing, when a man came running up to me and told me that someone was trapped in the men's rest room and screaming. I got there as quickly as possible and heard the screaming. Luckily, one of the portholes was cracked open. I slowly pushed it open far enough to see a young man that was maybe in his twenties. He had entered the bathroom and locked the door behind him. When he tried to leave, he had forgotten that he had locked the door. It appeared to me that maybe he had a learning disability of some sort. Most anyone feels a sense of panic when they feel trapped. I began to get his attention and calm him down by talking gently to him. Once the panic seemed to be leaving him, I got him to try to turn the lock left, and then right until it moved. I told him that the door would be moving a little and not to worry. I had gotten the guy that called this to my attention, to gently push and pull on the door from the outside until the force was off of the locking mechanism. The latch clicked on the young man's second try, and the door came open with the help of the man on the outside. As the young man came out, he asked me if I was the man at the window. I told him yes, and he had done a good job getting the lock unhung. He thanked me and hugged me. He quickly left to go to the car where his family was.

That most sincere hug from him, made me feel accomplished that day. Somehow, I had managed to calm him down and be the force that he needed at that moment. The joy of helping someone is all we need at times, to help us feel better about ourselves. He was my gift that day. Thank you, God.

Chapter 18

How Did You Do That?

On a pleasant Saturday afternoon in the fall, we had been stacking and packing every car we could on each load. Both boats have four lanes, but at the very back we will load the last few in odd positions to maximize the space while giving people the room to get out. Our Mate had told the driver to watch me carefully and do what I told her. I approached the driver's window and instructed her to watch me and not the fenders of the car. I assured her that there was not a rush, and not to worry. All she needed to do was totally trust me, and watch my hand signals. I told her to keep the brake pedal covered, and she would be fine. She slowly advanced, and I pointed her hard towards the port side rail. I used both hands to stop her about four inches from the metal wall, and signaled her to stay still and turn the wheel hard away from the wall to the right. Once she had the wheels turned to lock, I had her ease off the brake and pull forward about six feet. I stopped her and told her to place her emergency brake on, and turn off the car. I then smiled at her and told her she had done a great job. It took under a minute to get her and the car to this point.

I then quickly helped Mate Coby Benson and another deckhand pull the safety cargo netting into place, and hook the safety line across the deck. When I turned around, I was confronted by a man that I would soon discover was the husband of the woman I had just guided into place. He, and a buddy of his had gotten out of the back seat and made their way to me. The two women were standing behind them giggling like teenagers. He said, "How did you do that?" I really didn't know exactly what he meant, so I asked him, "How did I do what?"

That is when his expression changed to a huge smile, and honestly I began to breathe normal again. He had seemed so serious, that I was a bit worried. Then he proclaimed that he had been married to her for fifteen years, and she had never listened as intently to his directions as she did to mine. She thanked me repeatedly, as he informed me that he had no idea that they would make it onto the ferry. I felt it time to thank her again for listening to my directions and trusting some old guy that she had never seen before in her life. I told them that the key was getting people to trust us with their cars. We don't want to see people get their paint scratched. It really gets back to what I talked about earlier in the book. It is about the driver's willingness to give control to a stranger. These two couples from upstate, had ventured out to tour Southport and ride the ferry, while on a weekend trip to the coast. During a chance encounter, and a very short time, they had turned me into their newest friend. They shared laughs and heartfelt appreciation with me. In fact, the husband offered me a six pack of beer as a reward for my assistance. I explained to him how grateful I was, but I could not accept it.

Just to complete this tale with full disclosure, we got 36 vehicles, two motorcycles, and several bicycles on that load. So yes, we had a load!

right: port rail heading to Southport

Chapter 19

The Wedding

This tale occurred on the M/V *Fort Fisher*, and I must give credit, where credit is due. It happened while I was part of the "pool", and not yet assigned to either ferry permanently. It was a beautiful Saturday, and a passenger walked up to me and asked if we were going to do anything different for the wedding party that afternoon. I had not heard anything about a wedding party, so I went straight to the wheelhouse and talked to the Captain. He too was clueless. After making a call to the terminal, we found out the story.

There are no provisions or precedents for renting a State owned ferry for a private affair, such as a wedding. The groom had called to try to get this arranged, only to find out the bad news portion of his request. Alas, there was a good news portion also. All they had to do was get the entire wedding party staged on the Fort Fisher side, where they wanted to start, and see how much of a boatload they were going to make up. Once assembled, their entire party did not fill up the boat. They then bought three extra tickets, so they could leave three spaces empty at the front to hold the ceremony. When all was loaded, we still loaded about ten cars that were not part of the wedding group. For the price of three tickets, fifteen dollars, they had accomplished having their wedding on the ferry.

The bride had decided that this was where she wanted to get married, because this is where he proposed to her. The couple was from the Raleigh area, and had ridden the ferry for her first time ever, right after they met. She loved the ride so much, that she was determined to make it part of their history together. Most of her family was from Canada, and they came down for the event. Immediately upon leaving the Fort Fisher ramp, everyone got out of their cars, and gathered at the front of the ferry for the ceremony. They successfully completed the ceremony within the crossing time. Even the passengers that were not part of the wedding, enjoyed the event. They took pictures, so they could share their surprise attendance with their families and friends back home. The wedding party left the ferry on the Southport side and ventured into town to have their

reception at one of the waterfront restaurants. Later that day, many of the group returned to ride back to the Fort Fisher side, where they were staying for the weekend. Everything turned out well for the couple, and for us. This was just another example of why this job is rewarding. To be able to be part of such an impromptu event, that will last forever in someone's memory and photo album. I hope the couple has a lovely cruise through life.

Chapter 20

The
Ferry Crews

As a short time employee of only a few years, there is something important to consider about this job. It is an honest and honorable profession with an astounding history. It provides daily challenges, while not inundating one with relentless pressure. Let's face reality here. Bumping a piling or cluster too hard, or gently rubbing bottom is not equivalent to crashing the plane. But there will be paperwork! All positions aboard the boats require constant attention to some degree. Adjustments have to be made occasionally at all job levels.

When the Mate or Captain is at the wheel, they have to anticipate the actions of other vessels on the water. Our Captain Marybeth Ray has a good saying pertaining to the carelessness of some private vessel Captains. "Just because you can afford to own a boat doesn't mean you should be allowed to pilot it." We have had private boats worth several million dollars, cut in front of us, missing a collision by as close as fifty feet. Many boat owners count on everything working correctly all the time. If you have ever been around boats at all, you should know differently. You have to allow for error in judgement, or equipment failure at any moment.

Every crew member position has certain knowledge requirements that must be met. Some positions require a USCG issued license. Different size boats and ships, along with their location of operation, will determine the type of license required. Along with the tests that must be taken, comes time in grade actual hands-on training. Pre-requisite training and testing has a sizable cost associated with it. Don't think a few dollars, instead think hundreds, if not thousands. By the time you add in the classroom cost, motel fees, and travel expenses, you have made quite an investment in your future. It may not add up to the cost of tuition at a university for a four year degree, but it takes some planning. This is even more difficult if you're young and starting a family. Since these licenses become the property of the licensee, most employers, including the NCDOT Ferry Division does not reimburse or pay any portion of this expense. Like I said earlier, you've got to love this type of work.

Each of us in the "working world" should compare our tasks, with what others go through, before we start complaining. Think about the police officer that puts on a bullet proof vest at the beginning of each shift, hoping it won't be needed. How about the nurses that wait on patients hand and foot, while their supervisors are wondering where they are. These are the people that clean up the messy diapers and sheets of our loved ones that can no longer control themselves. Think of the field hands that do back breaking labor, just for a chance to make a new and better life for their families. Is your job looking better? None of these jobs pay what the task is worth. The pay and the situational environment is based on whatever amount the market will bear. If you start comparing the wages of these type jobs to the income of the professional sports player or A-list entertainer, you are destined to depress yourself. What we can do, is be sure to thank all of these people. Perhaps you could even give them a hug, or a better deal on the used car that you are selling. They will appreciate it.

right top: Capt. Marybeth Ray gives the Mate Bars to newly appointed Mate, Coby Benson
right bottom: chocks secure the wheels of the first and last vehicle in each lane

Chapter 21

The 2017 Crew
of the M/V *Southport*

The reason I want to dedicate a chapter to the crew of the M/V *Southport* is because it is the crew that I am a part of. They existed is some form before I ever got here, and will exist after I am gone. But it is the team that gave you this story. Without the attitude of the crew as a whole, I wouldn't be so positive and passionate about this job. The crew is a blend of young to old, with a tremendous number of years' experience among them. I don't think that I have ever heard anyone, employees or passengers, complain about any individual on this crew. It is a dedicated collection of ferry sailors. So as they say, let me introduce the band!

Captain Marybeth Ray is from Southport, NC. Her qualifications include 1600 Ton Ocean, Radar unlimited, 50 Ton Auxiliary Sail Vessels, Able Seaman-Any Waters, Unlimited Lifeboatman. She was born in Beaufort, SC into a US Marine Corp family. She spent her years between 12 and 35 on Andros Island, Bahama where her boating career began. She loves teaching and sharing her vast knowledge of boats and life on the water. She has been an inspiration to me as a Ferry Division employee. She has many friends that travel the ferry on occasion and will ask us to let them say hello to her if possible. That really tells the tale of what type of person she is.

Captain Chad Bond is from Belhaven, NC. He has a 1600 Ton Inland, and a Six Pack Near Shore license. Chad earned a BA degree in Business Administration from East Carolina University in Greenville, NC. He owns several boats that he uses for commercial fishing and fun. He is a true "downeastern" North Carolina family man.

Chief Engineer Bob Hanrahan lives in Knoxville, Tennessee. He was born and raised on Staten Island in New York. He retired from the Staten Island Ferry System before coming south to work with us. Bob has embraced the south and enjoys all it has to offer. His love of wildlife brings out the happiest moments for him. Bob was in his glory when he assisted in the rescue of an injured pelican. I don't think a childhood Christmas memory could have surpassed that moment for him.

Chief Engineer Tony Milicia lives with his wife near Morehead City, NC. He hails from Maxton, NC in the Sandhill area. He is retired USCG. Tony has traveled the world during his career. His show of respect to all passengers is a trait that will not go unnoticed by anyone. I know in my mind, that Tony was the kid in school that always got the comment on his report card "Plays well with others".

Oiler Chris Pittman lives with his wife and three kids in Southport, NC. He was raised in the Morehead City, NC area. Chris will very soon be testing for his Chief Engineer license. He is also a chef and manager at one of Southport's barbeque restaurants on his days off. He is a focused young man that any parent would be proud of. If you ask him what job he is most proud of, he will say husband and father.

Mate Coby Benson lives in Caswell Beach, NC on Oak Island. He was raised in Nashville, TN. and Wilmington, NC. Coby tested for his Mate's license in July of 2017 in Houston, Texas and attained a perfect score of 100 on the majority of the sections for this license. He has also served part time as a crew member, on the R/V (Research Vessel) *Cape Hatteras*, owned by Cape Fear Community College. Coby comes from a close-knit family, although they are spread out. When I look at Coby, I see a young man that I would be proud to go into any battle with. He is sincere and trustworthy to a fault. Coby is slow to judge and quick to analyze. He will go far in this profession.

Deckhand Larry Modlin lives with his wife Jennifer, in Southport, NC. Yes, this is me, so I will not use third person language. I haven't been diagnosed with that disorder yet. I was born and raised in Jamesville, NC. I am a proud graduate of the University of Margaritaville. I attended East Carolina University in Greenville, NC on a basketball scholarship where I discovered that 6'7" was not that tall, in Division One ball. If you look me up, I WILL NOT be in the basketball records. Let's just say my hoop career was short, and less than outstanding. I did play my heart out. It was a real honor to play with, and against, some of the players that I did.

Front: Captain Chad Bond, Captain Marybeth Ray, Chief Engineer Tony Milicia
Back: Mate Coby Benson, Chief Engineer Bob Hanrahan,
Oiler Chris Pittman, and Deckhand Larry Modlin

Epilogue

I sincerely hope that I have brought a little laughter to some of you. That is a reward to me, especially when it is so tough to find true humor now. It seems so wrong to go for the laughs at another's expense. The world seems to be full of bullies and narcissists. It is really hard to find the pleasures of life at times. That is why I have worked diligently at giving people a reason to cherish the little blessings, if it is nothing but a friendly smile at someone you've never before seen.

These tales from the ferry amount to a collection gathered from only three years, and all but one took place with one crew. There are many more boats in the North Carolina Ferry Division, at several other crossings. Many years have passed since the first ferry took the first vehicle across. Imagine all the tales that could be told! Many crews have served together for years aboard these boats. I truly feel that each member holds their own level of pride in what they have done. Every day is not always the best for each of us, so as I have asked earlier, please forgive us if we at times answer too quickly or seem abrupt. That is not our normal, at least for most of us.

Cape Fear Ferry Tales is just a small collection of stories and information that I thought some people may be interested in. I tried to share some of my philosophies, without sounding too preachy. There were other encounters that I could have told you about. I chose not to elaborate on those, because I felt they were perhaps from a point of view that everyone may not understand. I have been hurt at times in life because I trusted too much, either in the wrong thing, or at the wrong time. That is the price we pay for being part of this civilization riding this rock around the sun. I had rather be hurt from trusting too much, than to hurt someone else by not trusting at all. By risking a little at times, I have been greatly rewarded. When you take just a few minutes to acknowledge someone, and assist them with something when they don't expect you to, it shows them respect. When someone that can hardly speak your language leans in to you, and says thank you, along with a firm handshake, a rush comes over you that you probably don't get often enough. This makes the world a better place.

I certainly didn't pen this with dreams of making huge amounts of money. The old adage goes, "if you can't be rich, be famous". In my life, I have found that it is relatively easy to be famous. It just may not always be a good thing that you are famous for. This little book will not make me famous by some standards. Yet, if just a few of you remember me for it, then that will be famous enough for me.

My plan at present is to remain a member of this crew aboard the M/V *Southport*. We have just had the boat returned to us after an eleven month absence. It has been in our shipyard in Manns Harbor, NC getting its USCG required hull inspection. During this time, the boat engines and support systems have been overhauled and updated. The entire wheelhouse got an update with new pilot stations and controls. The boat also has a new paint job. So now, the white is really white, and the Duke blue is a true Duke blue again. I hope to see you aboard soon.

Acknowledgments

I sincerely want to thank our patrons, commuters, and tourists. You gave me these tales and made my life better by smiling at our crew.

My Mom and Dad have gone on to their next destination. Without them, I would not be me. Jack and Hester Modlin taught me how to look for the beauty in this world, and how to treat others. They took me on my first ferry ride, and taught me to look out of the window when traveling by car. Dad would say, "Don't miss a thing, we may never come back this way."

My wife, Jennifer, gives me a reason to be better every day. She stands beside me in life's trials, and helps me to pick my battles. It would be hard to find a better travel companion, or a prettier woman inside and out.

My heart goes out to the crew of the M/V *Southport* under the command of Captain Marybeth Ray. We strive to be a team while no member tries to be the star. I sincerely thank each one of them for accepting me as I am, and letting me be part of this crew. No crew stays together permanently. The crews seem to be in a constant state of flux due to the need to put the right people in the right place. I'll be sad when that day comes. At my age, I've grown to appreciate consistency.

I want to thank Phil Blount. Phil has been a friend since childhood. He was my first Captain, in Little League Baseball and then High School Basketball. He was, and still is, always there with a word of encouragement. He is the owner and President of Icons Inc. in Charlotte, NC.

I bow in honor to that funny lady in Wilmington, NC, that writes so well, Celia Rivenbark. Her observational humor has made me laugh, and inspired me to put this little book together. She is an icon for all women, not just southern born and bred.

Homage must be paid to Jimmy Buffett. He provided the sound track for my survival, and stands firmly on a shared platform of perspective. I will always be indebted to him for more than he'll ever know.

Fincannon and Associates came into my life around 1985. Mark, Craig, and Lisa, along with all the "associates" over the years, have worked hard to build their agency into what it is today. They have also contributed and dedicated themselves to keeping the film industry strong and alive in the Wilmington area, as well as over the southeast U.S. They are an anchor to the film and arts community in Wilmington.

I would also like to sincerely thank David Lewis of Wilmington, NC for his friendship and leadership over the years. For many years I served as Public Works Director under David, when he was the City Manager of the City of Boiling Spring Lakes, NC. He was a master at taking a beat to process all information possible before making a decision. David made every employee serving under him feel important. He is a fountain of encouragement to me

The facts that I have stated in this book about certain historical events have been given to you for thought and enticement. Please feel free to look into the facts and history more intently. I collected my information from the NCDOT Ferry Division website, local historical printings, family notebooks, and other information handed down to me from the other crew members. I usually tried to verify these hand-me-down stories by checking printed and vetted material. I do want to mention a book that was given to me by my mother, Hester Anne Swain Modlin. It is titled; *Swains of Nantucket, Tales and Trails*. It was written by Robert H. Swain and published in 1990.

Viking history and culture is very difficult to verify, due to their practice of not writing anything down. They had no historians or record keepers. The Viking culture has a huge influence on all of us, to this very day. We can thank the archeologist and other cultures for what information we do have. The reason I mention this is simple, but important. No matter how unimportant you may feel that your family history is, take the time to write down what you know. Somewhere in the future, a descendant may look back for a linchpin that took them to where they are. You may be that important piece they are looking for.

I close with this wish for each of you. Sail on through life, and cherish each moment. Choose your crew wisely. They need to be able to stay with you, in the good weather and through the bad. Commit yourself to the ones in your life that have been given to you as a gift from above. Persevere through the difficult course that must be taken at times. Not quitting is the biggest part of the battle. Remember, you may not win every battle, but you can still win the war.

I sincerely hope each of you find your "One Particular Harbor". Sail on, and stay true to yourself. Look for the shade of the "Lone Palm" and smile at all those who pass by. We only get one Earth and one life, so let us take care and enjoy both. Remember to listen to your Captain!

Sincerely,

Larry Modlin